BECOME A
PLUMBER

by Kate Conley

BrightPoint Press

San Diego, CA

BrightPoint Press

© 2021 BrightPoint Press
an imprint of ReferencePoint Press, Inc.
Printed in the United States

For more information, contact:
BrightPoint Press
PO Box 27779
San Diego, CA 92198
www.BrightPointPress.com

LIBRARY OF CONGRESS CATALOGING-IN-PUBLICATION DATA

Names: Conley, Kate A., 1977- author.
Title: Become a plumber / by Kate Conley.
Description: San Diego : ReferencePoint Press, 2021. | Series: Skilled and vocational trades | Includes bibliographical references and index. | Audience: Grades 10-12.
Identifiers: LCCN 2020003752 (print) | LCCN 2020003753 (eBook) | ISBN 9781678200145 (hardcover) | ISBN 9781678200152 (eBook)
Subjects: LCSH: Plumbers--Juvenile literature. | Plumbing--Vocational guidance--Juvenile literature.
Classification: LCC HD8039.P6 C66 2020 (print) | LCC HD8039.P6 (eBook) | DDC 696/.1023--dc23
LC record available at https://lccn.loc.gov/2020003752
LC eBook record available at https://lccn.loc.gov/2020003753

CONTENTS

AT A GLANCE

- Plumbers put in and maintain plumbing systems.

- Plumbers install plumbing fixtures, such as faucets. They install appliances such as dishwashers and water heaters.

- Plumbers work in different settings. These include new construction sites and homes.

- Plumbers make sure people have clean water every day.

- Plumbers train as apprentices. Training often lasts between four and five years.

- At the end of their training, students take an exam. If they pass, they earn a plumbing license.

- Most plumbers have good math skills. They are good at working with their hands. They know how to provide good customer service to clients.

- Plumbers usually work full-time hours. They may be on call. This means they are ready to take care of plumbing emergencies. Emergencies may happen on evenings and weekends.

- Plumber jobs are expected to increase by 14 percent between 2018 and 2028.

- People today are becoming more interested in green building methods. These methods save water. The growing interest creates new jobs for plumbers.

WHY BECOME A PLUMBER?

Some people think of a plumber as someone "bent over a clogged toilet with a plunger," says Fred Schilling. "Nothing could be further from reality!"[1] Schilling trained as a plumber in the military. He later was one of the youngest people to become a master plumber in Florida. Today, he owns a plumbing business.

Plumbers fix and install pipes. Pipes transfer water and other materials into buildings.

Plumbers do unclog toilets. But a

plumber's job is more than that. "The

oxygen you receive in an operating

room . . . was installed by a plumber,"

says Schilling. "The gas ovens and stoves that prepare your dinner at your favorite restaurant were installed by a plumber."[2]

Half a million Americans work as plumbers. They install and maintain plumbing systems. Plumbing systems are networks of pipes. The pipes carry water, steam, air, or natural gas. They can be made of different materials. Some pipes are plastic. Others are made of metal such as copper, brass, or iron.

Plumbers' work provides water to homes, schools, and businesses. The work is important to public health. Plumbing

Pipes can come in many different sizes and materials.

systems bring clean, safe water to people.

People count on this whenever they turn

on a faucet. Plumbing also brings natural

gas to **appliances**. Appliances include gas

stoves and water heaters.

Plumbing is a trade. It is a skilled job

that requires years of training. Most of the

People rely on plumbers' unseen work.

training takes place on a job site.

A student works with a professional

plumber. The plumber teaches the student

how to do plumbing work. Students learn

in a real-world setting. Many students also

take classes. When they have completed

these steps, they can get a **license** to work

as a plumber.

The job outlook for plumbing is good. Many businesses need more plumbers. This means that finding work is not hard for most plumbers. Green construction is making more work for plumbers. More builders and homeowners want to **conserve** water. Plumbers can install systems to make this happen.

Much of plumbers' work goes unseen. It hides behind walls. It is buried underground. But plumbers are key to keeping a community working smoothly. They keep the nation's water supply clean, safe, and dependable.

CHAPTER ONE

WHAT DOES A PLUMBER DO?

P lumbers install pipes that carry water. They also repair these pipes. But the work plumbers do is much more than that. Every day, plumbers' work keeps the public safe. Water can carry diseases. These diseases can be deadly. Clean, safe water can be the difference between life and death.

Before modern plumbing, some cities built sewage tunnels. Often, waste from these tunnels was dumped into sources of drinking water.

Modern plumbing systems first began in cities around the 1840s. Before then, homes did not have running water. People carried water into their homes. When they were done, people then dumped

13

their dirty water. The dirty water made its way into lakes and rivers. This created a problem. It **contaminated** the lakes and rivers. These bodies of water were sources of drinking water. The dirty drinking water led to illnesses.

Illnesses that spread through dirty water killed thousands of people every year. People wanted to stop the spread of illnesses. They needed a way to keep dirty and clean water separate. So cities began installing plumbing systems. This created a demand for plumbing experts. The result was a new job: the plumber.

Some pipes are color coded. A plumber must connect pipes in new buildings to the correct systems.

INSTALLING PLUMBING SYSTEMS

Today, plumbers havc many duties. One

of them is to install plumbing systems in

new buildings. Most of a plumbing system

is hidden behind walls. But it is important.

A good plumbing system supplies water to

Some cities use water towers to store their water supply.

faucets and appliances. It also drains water that is unclean.

For a building to have running water, a plumber must connect it to a water supply. Water that enters a building from a water supply is clean and safe. It can be used for drinking, cooking, and bathing. Most cities oversee the water supply for their citizens. Cities store the water in massive tanks. It then flows through large, underground pipes. These pipes are called water mains. Plumbers connect new buildings to water mains.

Water that enters a building must leave it too. Water drains from sinks, toilets, and tubs. Drained water is called wastewater. It has bits of food, soap, oils, and human waste in it. Plumbers connect wastewater pipes to large sewage pipes. These are underground. They carry the wastewater to a treatment plant. Some homes are in rural areas. They may not have access to a sewage system. In that case, plumbers connect a home's wastewater to a septic tank. It is a large storage tank that is buried on a homeowner's property. The tank stores the home's wastewater.

WATER TREATMENT PLANTS

At a treatment plant, wastewater goes through several steps. Screens remove solid matter from the water. Sand and dirt sink to the bottom. Then bacteria consume animal or plant matter in the wastewater. Next, chlorine is added to the water. This kills the bacteria. Finally, the chlorine is removed. The water is returned to rivers, lakes, and oceans.

After connecting a building to a water main and a sewage system, plumbers begin the next step. They install the pipes. These pipes supply and drain water throughout the building. This step is called the rough-in. It happens once the building's frame is in place but before the walls go up. Plumbers and other workers have easy access to all parts of the building. When the walls go up, much of the plumbing work will be hidden from view.

During the job, plumbers use blueprints. These plans say where plumbing systems need to be placed. Plumbers select the right pipes for the job. For example, a

plumber installing a wastewater line would

use plastic pipes. A plumber installing

a gas line would use black iron pipes.

Plumbers measure and mark out where

each pipe will go. Then they begin the

installation. Plumbers use tools such as

pipe benders, pipe cutters, and hand saws

to do the job. They may also use torches to

weld pipes together.

The final step is adding **fixtures**

and appliances. Fixtures allow people

to access a building's water supply.

Examples of fixtures are faucets, toilets,

Drinking fountains are a kind of fixture.

and showerheads. Appliances are

machines that do a specific job. Plumbers

install appliances such as water heaters,

water softeners, and dishwashers.

Plumbers may use glue to connect plastic pipes.

SPECIALIZED PLUMBERS

Plumbers install more than just water pipes. Sometimes plumbing systems must carry other types of liquids and gases.

These substances require extra care. Plumbers who work with them have specialized training. Most of these plumbers also have years of experience.

One substance plumbers commonly work with is natural gas. Natural gas is a fuel. It flows through pipes. It powers stoves, furnaces, and water heaters.

PIPEFITTERS

Pipefitters are specialized plumbers. They do not work in homes or offices. They work on large-scale industrial sites. Pipefitters commonly work in factories. They install and maintain pipes. These pipes carry chemicals. Other pipefitters work on underground pipelines. These pipelines carry natural gas or oil over long distances.

Natural gas is a clean, affordable way to power these appliances. But working with it can be dangerous. Natural gas is highly **flammable**. Plumbers who work with it must follow safety rules closely.

Some plumbers work with medical gases. These gases are used in hospitals and clinics. Examples of these gases are oxygen and nitrogen. Plumbers connect the gases' sources to a system of pipes. The pipes carry the gases to operating and patient rooms. Safe delivery of these gases can save lives.

Plumbers connect the pipes that bring natural gas to appliances. Natural gas heats many homes.

Other plumbers install sprinkler systems. In many states, laws require new buildings to have sprinkler systems. These can detect heat or smoke from a fire. When this happens, water flows through the sprinkler heads. A sprinkler system can put out flames quickly and save lives.

MAINTAINING PLUMBING SYSTEMS

Not all plumbers work on new buildings. Some maintain plumbing systems that already exist. They travel to homes and buildings on service calls. Sometimes a service call is a small job, such as installing a new faucet. Other times, the job may be

Plumbers can fix problems ranging from leaky faucets to broken water mains.

more difficult. For example, a plumber may

have to wade through water to find the

source of a leak.

This work requires plumbers to have

good problem-solving skills. It also requires

them to know how to fix the problem once

they identify it. Often, service calls come from people who are panicked. They may have a leak flooding their basement. Sewage may be backing up into their drains. These are emergency service calls. The plumber must act quickly to prevent further damage.

Many plumbers find this type of service call to be a rewarding part of the job. Roger Wakefield is a master plumber. He recalls one of his emergency calls. It was from a woman who had sewage coming up into her house. "I show up, and she's crying," Wakefield says. "I looked at her and

Plumbers work hard to take care of their clients.

said, 'Ma'am, look, everything is gonna be okay. I can take care of this.'" He identified the problem. Then he repaired it. The client was relieved. Wakefield was pleased he could help. "Taking care of people is a great thing," he says.[3]

CHAPTER TWO

WHAT TRAINING DO PLUMBERS NEED?

To become plumbers, students undergo several years of training. Each state has different requirements. But all plumbers must be at least eighteen years old. They must also have a high school diploma. Or they can take a General Education Development (GED) test. Passing the

Some states, such as Alabama, require only two years of training. Others, such as Montana, require five.

GED test shows that someone has a high school level of education. If students meet these requirements, they can apply to be apprentices.

Apprentices are taught by experts in plumbing.

APPRENTICE PLUMBERS

Apprentices receive their training on the job.

They work full-time. That is typically forty

to fifty hours a week. Licensed plumbers

supervise them. During their training,

apprentices earn wages. They usually earn about half of what a licensed plumber earns. Some apprenticeships are offered through local plumbing businesses. Others are through a union. A union is an organized group of workers. Its members make decisions about their trade. They focus on topics such as safety guidelines and hourly wages. Apprenticeships often last between four and five years.

"The trade is so much more than hanging pipe, unblocking drains. This is where an apprenticeship comes in," says Michael O'Brien. He is president of a plumbing and heating company. Apprenticeships allow experienced plumbers to pass on their knowledge to new plumbers. "I did a five-year apprenticeship back in 1983," says O'Brien. "It's been the best thing I've ever done for myself."[4] O'Brien finds it exciting to

WOMEN IN PLUMBING

In 2019, only 2.7 percent of all US plumbers were women. That is slowly changing. Organizations of tradeswomen visit schools. They talk to girls about trades. Mary Ann Naylor works for Oregon Tradeswomen. She says, "If girls get the opportunity to see all these workshops . . . led by journeywomen, . . . talk to women doing these careers, [and] try the tools themselves, it demystifies it for them."

Quoted in Hal Conick, "Why Are There Still So Few Women in Plumbing?" Contractor, February 6, 2015. www.contractormag.com.

give his apprentices the same opportunity and watch them succeed.

One of O'Brien's apprentices is Eric Becker. "My apprenticeship is amazing," says Becker. "You get to use your brain a lot. And you're always problem-solving; you're always thinking on your toes. It's never the same, and I really enjoy that aspect of it," says Becker. "It's a short journey for the payoff you get in the end."[5]

TIME IN THE CLASSROOM

Apprentices often spend time in the classroom. Many states require apprentices to take classes. These classes are part

Apprentices take classes so they can have a strong understanding of system designs and functions.

of their training. Apprentices study topics

that apply to their work. For example,

apprentices might take math classes.

The math is specifically for plumbers.

Apprentices learn skills such as calculating

the volume of water that a pipe can safely carry.

Dean Petersen is a plumbing instructor in Wisconsin. Petersen teaches his students to learn beyond on-the-job training. "We teach them theory, . . . code, . . . and then how . . . we tie this all together in system design," says Petersen.[6] Theory is the basics of plumbing work. Codes are the guidelines plumbers must follow for safety. Knowing these elements allows plumbers to do their work.

The students also get to spend some time in a lab. It gives them a chance to practice hands-on skills. Then they can be ready for work on a real job site. A lab gives them a safe place to practice. They can learn from mistakes and ask questions.

JOURNEY WORKER PLUMBERS

Plumbing apprenticeships vary by state. But most have the same elements. For example, an apprenticeship may require 8,000 hours on the job and 500 hours in the classroom. Then the next step is to get a license. An apprentice takes a test. This test proves his or her plumbing knowledge.

Students who pass the exam earn their licenses. They become journey worker

Journey worker plumbers can do some work by themselves without supervision. They can install new appliances and make repairs.

plumbers. Journey workers can work on

job sites. They do not always need direct

supervision. They can work on a variety

of jobs from new construction to home

service calls. Some states may limit what

kinds of work journey workers can do.

Others may require them to work under master plumbers.

Journey worker plumbers may be self-employed or work for a company. Self-employed journey workers can pick the jobs they want. They can set their own hours. Other journey workers work for plumbing companies. They take the jobs assigned to them. In 2018, the median national salary for plumbers was $53,910 per year.

MASTER PLUMBERS

Some plumbers remain journey workers for their entire careers. Others wish to go

Master plumbers can manage other plumbers. They may have journey workers and apprentices working for them.

further. They become master plumbers.

Master plumbers have several years of

experience. They can **bid** on jobs, manage

projects, and supervise apprentices.

They can also design plumbing systems.

Masters usually earn higher salaries than

journey workers do. The median salary for

master plumbers is closer to $60,000.

The requirements to become a master

plumber vary by state. But typically, a

plumber must have logged several years

MORE THAN JUST A JOB

Frank Tumbarello is a master plumber.
He has worked as a plumber for many years.
Eventually, he came "to realize that it's more
than just a job but a whole way of life."
Tumbarello feels like he is "part of a tradition of
craftsmen that goes back hundreds of years."

Quoted in "Meet a Plumber," Explore the Trades, n.d.
https://explorethetrades.org.

working under a master plumber. They must also take an exam. Usually, one part of the exam is written. The other is a practical exam. It allows plumbers to show their skills with different types of piping.

Whether master or journey worker, many plumbers enjoy their jobs. Their years of apprenticeship gave them a skill that is in high demand. The plumbing trade helps keep communities safe and running smoothly. Many plumbers take great pleasure in knowing their work makes this happen.

WHAT IS LIFE LIKE AS A PLUMBER?

Life as a plumber is filled with variety. Many plumbers like this. They never know where the job will take them. "There's no such thing as a 'typical' day for me, because no two days are ever the same," says plumber Jessie Cannizzaro. "I'm a licensed plumber, but I wear a hat for everything so I can fill in wherever

Plumbers must be ready to respond to emergencies. They might have to work on weekends or late at night.

I'm needed."[7] For example, she might

spend a day planning future jobs. Or she

might spend an evening responding to an

emergency call.

HOURS AND EMPLOYERS

Most plumbers work full-time. They schedule forty to fifty hours of work. But not all plumbing jobs fall neatly into a schedule. A pipe might burst in the middle of the night. A gas line might spring a leak on a weekend. These are plumbing emergencies. To handle them, plumbers take turns being on call. An on-call plumber goes to an emergency job no matter the day or the time.

More than 60 percent of plumbers work for contractors. Contractors are plumbers who own their own business. They bid on

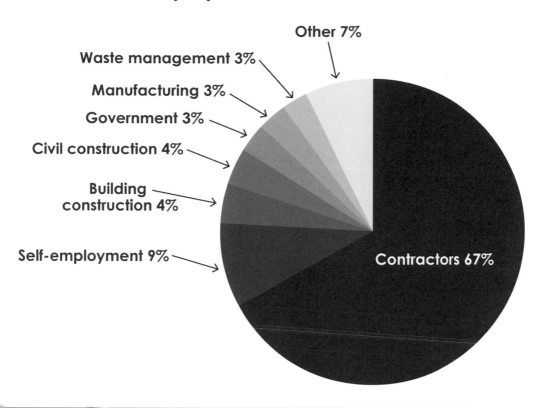

Employers of Plumbers in 2018

- Other 7%
- Waste management 3%
- Manufacturing 3%
- Government 3%
- Civil construction 4%
- Building construction 4%
- Self-employment 9%
- Contractors 67%

US Bureau of Labor Statistics, "Plumbers, Pipefitters, and Steamfitters: Employment by Industry, Occupation, and Percent Distribution, 2018 and Projected 2028," Employment Projections, US Department of Labor, n.d. https://data.bls.gov.

plumbing jobs. If they win a bid, contractors

send their plumbers to the site to work.

Plumbers who do not work for contractors

have other options. They can work directly for a business such as a factory or a hospital. They build and maintain plumbing systems for these businesses.

In 2018, nearly 10 percent of plumbers in the United States were self-employed. Some plumbers enjoy this a great deal.

CONTINUING EDUCATION

Plumbers must continue their education. This lets them keep their licenses. Each state has different rules. But most require several hours of classes. In some states, licensed plumbers must complete sixteen hours of training. They do this every two years. Of that, eight hours must relate to plumbing codes. Continuing education keeps plumbers on top of new developments in the trade.

It gives them flexibility. They can choose which jobs to take. They can also decide how many hours they work each day. But self-employment also comes with extra work. In addition to plumbing skills, plumbers must know how to run a business. They have to understand accounting, taxes, and insurance.

COMMON TRAITS OF PLUMBERS

Most plumbers share many traits. They are often physically fit. This helps because the job can be physically demanding. Plumbers often spend most of their workdays on their feet. They have to carry heavy

Plumbers might have to crouch or work in small spaces to get the job done.

equipment and tools. They may have to

climb ladders. Or they may have to lie on

their backs to access pipes. They must

also be good at working with their hands.

That is because they work with tools and

plumbing supplies.

Most plumbers are also good problem

solvers. They can look at a building's

PIPE MATERIALS

Plumbers must know what materials to use for each job. They use different types of pipes. PVC pipes are made of hard plastic. Plumbers often use them for wastewater. Water supply pipes can be made of metal. They may also be made of flexible plastic called PEX. Plumbers must know how to work with the different materials.

plumbing system and figure out what is causing a problem. Then they apply their skills to fix it. Most plumbing problems have several solutions. What works well on one job may not work well at a different site. Plumbers must think through each option. Then they decide which one is best.

Plumbers must be good at math. They work with fractions every day. They also convert units of measure. For example, they may switch between feet and inches. Geometry is another key math skill. For example, plumbers must understand angles to install a plumbing system. Plumbers

Plumbers need good communication skills. They must clearly explain different repair options.

commonly figure out area, volume, and perimeter. Plumbers also use math to bill clients. At each service call, a plumber calculates the cost of labor and parts used.

Successful plumbers are good at customer service. They listen closely when clients explain problems. They speak with clients clearly and respectfully. This is especially useful when explaining a repair and its costs. Good customer service includes respect for a job site. Plumbers keep their job sites as neat and tidy as possible.

RISKS OF THE JOB

Plumbers face risks every day. They might get injured. They could get ill. These risks for plumbers are higher than average. Water pressure is dangerous. Pipes may burst.

Plumbing tools can be dangerous if not used carefully and correctly.

They can throw water at 40 to 100 pounds

(18 to 45 kg) of pressure. This forces 200

to 400 gallons (757 to 1,514 L) of water out

of a pipe each minute. Plumbers risk facing

High-pressure water leaks can be dangerous for plumbers.

this head-on when repairing burst pipes.

It is like being hit with water from a hydrant.

Repairs can be dangerous. Plumbers

may encounter mold and lead. These

can cause long-term health problems.

Repairs involving sewage are also risky. Sewage can have dangerous fungi, parasites, and diseases. These are serious and sometimes deadly.

Plumbers face other daily risks. Steam from hot water pipes can cause burns. Working in cramped spaces may lead to pulled muscles. Plumbers might have to work in extreme weather. Job sites might have loud noises or flying **debris**. Plumbers could slip on wet surfaces. They could fall from ladders.

Plumbers must follow safety measures. Glasses protect their eyes. Earplugs or ear covers protect their hearing. Plumbers take frequent breaks when working in cramped spaces. Heavy gloves and long sleeves protect against cuts and burns. And slip-resistant boots help prevent falls.

Despite the risks, many plumbers enjoy the trade. It is a job that constantly challenges them. They can use their problem-solving skills. Each day brings different tasks. And working at a job site rather than sitting at a desk is a big perk. For many plumbers, these are some of the best parts of the job.

Plumbers wear safety equipment, such as thick gloves and goggles. These protect them from accidents and injuries.

CHAPTER FOUR

WHAT IS THE FUTURE FOR PLUMBERS?

The future for plumbers is promising. The Bureau of Labor Statistics (BLS) projects job growth. It estimates that plumber jobs will increase. Between 2018 and 2028, they will likely grow by 14 percent. This growth is faster than the average for all other jobs.

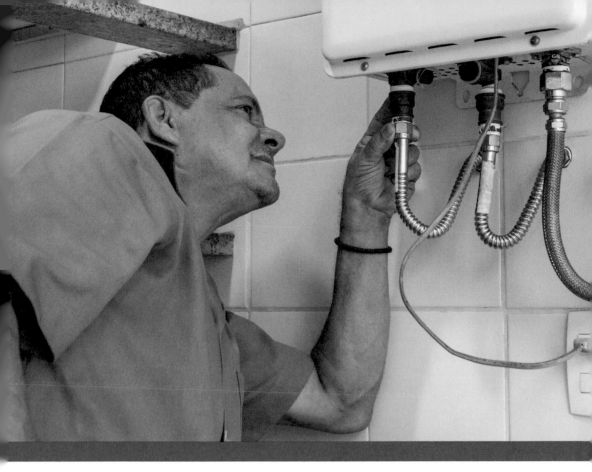

Plumbing is necessary for daily life. However, not many young people feel called to the profession.

THE PLUMBER SHORTAGE

High demand for plumbers is causing this

fast growth. Currently, there is a shortage

of plumbers. Contractors often do not

have enough licensed plumbers for all

their jobs. Then they must turn away jobs.

This shortage will continue to grow. That

is because plumbers are retiring. In 2018,

the average US plumber was around

HARVARD VS. PLUMBING SCHOOL

In 2013, Michael Bloomberg shined the spotlight on the plumbing trade. Bloomberg was the mayor of New York City. He spoke on a radio program about careers. He compared becoming a plumber to going to Harvard University. He said being a plumber "probably would be a better deal" than going to Harvard. That way a person does not spend "$40,000, $50,000 in tuition without earning income" for four years.

Quoted in Jennifer Fermino and Jonathan Lemire, "Skip College and Become a Plumber: Mayor Bloomberg," New York Daily News, May 17, 2013. www.nydailynews.com.

fifty-five years old. Many will retire in the next decade. Not enough new plumbers are being trained to take their places.

Many factors caused today's shortage of plumbers. In the past, children commonly followed in the footsteps of their parents. If a father worked as a plumber, his children would often do so too. But that has changed. For decades, few students have chosen the trades. They believed going to college would help them find a better job. But for many, that is not the case. They leave college with huge debt and few job prospects.

A career in the trades, such as plumbing, can be rewarding. Apprentices are paid to learn. They enter the workforce without debt. And with demand so high, plumbers and other trade workers can often earn high salaries fairly quickly. They also have good job security. "No matter how technologically advanced the world gets, plumbing is going to be . . . a basic necessity," says plumber Joseph Rosenblum.[8]

GROWING INDUSTRIES

One of the fastest-growing areas for plumbers is green construction. One of green construction's aims is to limit the

Plumbers can find many new opportunities in green construction.

resources buildings use. Plumbers can

install systems that reduce energy and

water usage. They install these systems in

new buildings. Or they put new systems into

existing buildings.

Dual-flush toilets can use up to 67 percent less water. They have two separate buttons that control how much water is used.

Many homeowners go green by using **efficient** fixtures. They hire plumbers to install these. Low-flow faucets use less water. Dual-flush toilets conserve water too. They have two different settings. One is for solid waste. The other is for liquid waste. These toilets can save many gallons of water each year. Plumbers also install water-saving dishwashers, washing machines, and hot water heaters.

GREEN WATER SYSTEMS

Plumbers may install green water systems. An example is gray water recycling. Gray water is water that has been gently used.

Gray water is clean enough to be reused for things like watering the lawn.

For that reason, it can be used again without being treated. Typically, gray water comes from washing machines. It also comes from bathroom sinks and bathtubs. It is not safe for drinking or cooking.

But it can be used in toilets. It can also

water lawns and crops.

Gray water systems save water and

money. They can reduce the amount of

water used outdoors by 40 percent. This

means a homeowner can have a lower

water bill each month. These systems are

SAVING WATER

Green plumbing saves water. Toilets use about
26 percent of a home's water. Switching to a
green toilet can save 13,392 gallons (50,694 L)
of water each year. Likewise, showers use
about 17 percent of a home's water. A low-flow
showerhead reduces water usage. Standard
heads use as much as 8 gallons (30 L) per
minute. But low-flow heads use as low as
1.6 gallons (6.1 L) per minute.

installed by plumbers. Plumbers know how to set up the systems. They keep gray water, drinking water, and wastewater separate. Failure to do this could result in a person becoming ill.

Plumbers can install systems that collect and reuse rainwater. These systems also help people save water. Storage tanks collect rainwater from roofs and drainpipes. Pumps move the rainwater in the tank to where it is needed. The rainwater is not safe to drink. But as with gray water, rainwater can be used for other purposes.

Rainwater collection systems are one way to save water.

OTHER DEVELOPMENTS

Green water systems are one way plumbing has changed recently. But it's not the only change. Plumbers now install cutting-edge fixtures, such as electronic toilets. They are using products that are safer for the environment. They use products like biosafe drain cleaners. These are safer than harsh chemicals. Plumbers also use new technology. For example, they can place small cameras into pipes. These cameras show where clogs and leaks are. Despite the changes, plumbers still do the same basic job. They make sure buildings

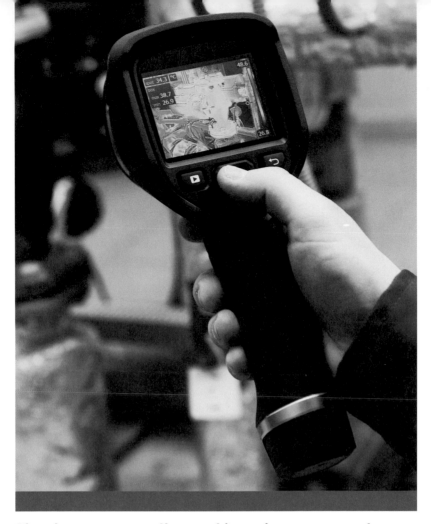

Plumbers can use thermal imaging cameras to spot problems with pipes.

have clean, safe water people can depend

on. And they install pipes that transport

necessary fuel. Their work will always be an

important part of communities.

GLOSSARY

appliances

machines, such as a dishwasher or washing machine, used to perform a specific task

bid

to offer to complete a job for a specific price

conserve

to use a resource carefully so it is not wasted

contaminated

made impure by adding an unsafe substance

debris

scattered, broken pieces of something that has been destroyed

efficient

producing a result with little or no waste

fixtures

equipment, such as faucets, permanently installed in a building

flammable

catching fire easily and burning quickly

license

legal permission to do something

SOURCE NOTES

INTRODUCTION: WHY BECOME A PLUMBER?

1. Quoted in Andy Orin, "Career Spotlight: What I Do as a Plumber," *Lifehacker*, February 24, 2016. https://lifehacker.com.

2. Quoted in Orin, "Career Spotlight."

CHAPTER 1: WHAT DOES A PLUMBER DO?

3. "Why I Love Being a Plumber," *YouTube*, uploaded by Roger Wakefield, January 9, 2019. www.youtube.com.

CHAPTER 2: WHAT TRAINING DO PLUMBERS NEED?

4. Quoted in "About Trades: Plumbing Apprentice," *YouTube*, uploaded by apprenticesearch, July 12, 2012. www.youtube.com.

5. Quoted in "About Trades."

6. Quoted in "Wisconsin Journeyman Plumber Testing & Licensing," *YouTube*, uploaded by BuildingWisconsinTV, May 4, 2017. www.youtube.com.

CHAPTER 3: WHAT IS LIFE LIKE AS A PLUMBER?

7. Quoted in Kathleen Green, "Interview with a Plumber," *Career Outlook* (blog), US Bureau of Labor Statistics, October 2016. www.bls.gov.

CHAPTER 4: WHAT IS THE FUTURE FOR PLUMBERS?

8. Quoted in Ann Carrns, "Sweet Smell of Money for Plumbers," *The New York Times*, March 24, 2014. www.nytimes.com.

RESEARCH

BOOKS

Emma Huddleston, *Plumbers on the Job*. Mankato, MN: The Child's World, 2020.

Wil Mara, *Be a Plumber*. Ann Arbor, MI: Cherry Lake Publishing, 2019.

Nathan Miloszewski, *Plumbers and Sewage Workers*. New York: PowerKids Press, 2019.

INTERNET SOURCES

Bureau of Labor Statistics, "Plumbers, Pipefitters, and Steamfitters," *Occupational Outlook Handbook*, US Department of Labor, September 4, 2019. www.bls.gov.

"How to Become a Plumber," *Explore the Trades*, n.d. https://explorethetrades.org.

"Water Treatment," *Water Education Foundation*, n.d. www.watereducation.org.

WEBSITES

Apprenticeship.gov
www.apprenticeship.gov

Apprenticeship.gov is a part of the US Department of Labor. This website provides information about apprenticeships. People can find and apply to apprenticeships through the website.

Plumbing-Heating-Cooling Contractors Association (PHCC)
www.phccweb.org

PHCC supports and trains tradespeople in the plumbing and HVAC industries. It has many resources and services for its members. Its members work in many different areas of the construction industry.

United Association (UA)
www.ua.org

The United Association of Journeymen and Apprentices of the Plumbing and Pipe Fitting Industry of the United States, Canada (UA) represents plumbers and people in plumbing-related trades. It is a union that provides training and certification.

INDEX

IMAGE CREDITS

ABOUT THE AUTHOR

Kate Conley has been writing nonfiction books for children for more than a decade. When she's not writing, Conley spends her time reading, drawing, and solving crossword puzzles. She lives in Minnesota with her husband and two children.